CONTENTS

What can astrology do for me? 2

What is astrology? 4

Your Sun sign 10

Your Rising sign 20

Your Moon sign 28

Elements 38

We are family 44

Best of friends 54

Your birthday log 64

Lucky in love 78

Life at school 86

WHAT CAN ASTROLOGY
do for me?

Astrology is a powerful tool for self-awareness. The idea that we are all connected – that the shifting energies of the Sun, Moon and planets above affect us here on Earth – is an ancient and philosophical belief. Astrology isn't fortune-telling – it can't predict your future and it doesn't deal in absolutes. It simply says that you are part of the universe around you, and by studying the stars, it's possible to learn more about yourself.

Why is this so important? Because the better understanding you have of your own inner make-up – your skills, your talents, your needs and your fears – the more insight you gain into why you act the way you do. And this gives you choices, empowering you to make changes and to build on your strengths. It makes it easier to feel confident and to accept yourself, quirks and all.

There are countless daily horoscopes in newspapers, magazines and online. But this book looks at more than just your star sign, which is only a small part of your personality picture. It helps you to find your Rising sign, which was appearing over the Eastern horizon at the time of your birth, and has a lot to tell you about the way others see you. You can also work out your Moon sign, which reveals the real you deep down inside, giving you the chance to get to grips with your innermost emotions, desires, fears and obsessions.

With a clearer picture of who you are, life becomes less complicated. Instead of trying to live up to others' expectations and being someone you're not, you can work instead on becoming the best version of yourself possible – someone who understands their talents and needs, who is perfectly unique and is happy.

What is
ASTROLOGY?

The stars and planets have always inspired a sense of wonder. The ancient peoples of Babylonia, Persia, Egypt, Greece and India were all fascinated by the cycles of the Moon, the rising and setting of the Sun, the position of the constellations and what it all meant. As these civilizations developed, they connected what they saw in the sky with the people and events on Earth, and astrology was born.

In ancient times, astrology was used to help monarchs rule. Kings and emperors would employ astrologers to predict the weather, speak to the gods and help manage the country.

Modern astrology has evolved to help ordinary people like you and me understand ourselves better – how we behave, how we feel about each other and how we can make the best of who we are.

THE SIGNS OF THE ZODIAC

Today we know that the planets revolve around the Sun, but astrology is based on how we see the solar system from here on Earth. The Zodiac is a group of 12 constellations that, from our viewpoint, seem to rotate around the Earth over the course of a year, like a huge wheel. These constellations are named after the animals and objects that our ancestors thought they looked most like – the ram, the lion, the scorpion and so on. Your Sun sign tells you which of the constellations the Sun was moving through on the day you were born. The signs have a natural order that never varies, beginning with Aries. The dates given on the right change slightly from year to year for the same reasons we have a leap year – each of our days is slightly longer than 24 hours. If you were born at the beginning or end of a sign, called 'the cusp', it's worth checking your Sun sign online to be sure.

ARIES	**LIBRA**
March 21–April 20	September 23–October 22
TAURUS	**SCORPIO**
April 21–May 21	October 23–November 21
GEMINI	**SAGITTARIUS**
May 22–June 21	November 22–December 21
CANCER	**CAPRICORN**
June 22–July 22	December 22–January 20
LEO	**AQUARIUS**
July 23–August 23	January 21–February 19
VIRGO	**PISCES**
August 24–September 22	February 20–March 20

THE FOUR ELEMENTS

*Each Sun sign is associated with one of four elements –
Fire, Earth, Air and Water.*

FIRE

Aries, Leo, Sagittarius
Fire signs are passionate, dynamic and temperamental.
They mix well with: Fire and Air types

EARTH

Taurus, Virgo, Capricorn
Earth signs are practical, cautious and reliable.
They mix well with: Water and Earth types

AIR

Gemini, Libra, Aquarius
Air signs are quick, curious and adventurous.
They mix well with: Air and Fire types

WATER

Cancer, Scorpio, Pisces
Water signs are sensitive, emotional and kind.
They mix well with: Earth and Water types

THE PLANETS

Astrology looks at the positions of the stars and planets at the time and place of your birth. The Sun and Moon aren't technically planets, but they're referred to that way by astrologers for ease of use. The Sun is a great place to start – it's the most important object in the solar system. Your Sun sign describes the essence of your identity, and says a great deal about your potential – the person you might become.

The position the Moon held in the sky at the time of your birth has a strong influence, too. It describes your emotions – how you feel deep inside. It can give you a better understanding of what you need to feel loved and cared for.

And there's also your Rising sign. This is the sign of the Zodiac that was appearing over the Eastern horizon at the time of your birth. It tells you more about how you interact with the world around you, especially to new situations. It's the filter through which you perceive the world and the impression you give to others on first meeting. Which means it's also how others often see you.

The positions of the other planets – Venus, Mercury, Mars, etc – in your birth chart all have their own effect. But these three taken together – Sun, Moon and Rising sign – will give you a deeper understanding of who you are and what you could become, your strengths and weaknesses, your real self.

Your SUN sign

ARIES

March 21–April 20

SYMBOL
The Ram

ELEMENT
Fire

RULING PLANET
Mars

BIRTHSTONE
Diamond

COLOUR
Red

BODY PART
Head

DAY OF THE WEEK
Tuesday

FLOWER
Honeysuckle

CHARACTER TRAITS
Brave, passionate, energetic, impatient

KEY PHRASE
'I am'

YOUR SUN SIGN

When people talk about astrology and ask about your star sign, they're referring to your Sun sign. It tells you which of the 12 constellations of the Zodiac the Sun was moving through on the day you were born. This makes it easy to work out, which is one of the reasons for its popularity. If you'd like to know the Sun sign of a friend or family member, the table on page 7 shows which days the Sun occupies each of the signs over the course of a year.

The Sun is the heart of your chart – it's the essence of who you are, and symbolizes the potential of what you can achieve. It's important to remember, though, that it is only a part of the whole picture when it comes to astrology. It's a wonderful starting point, but there are many other layers encasing your core identity, all of which affect the inner you.

ALL ABOUT YOU

Born with the Sun in Aries, you have the potential to help pioneer and begin things – your knowledge and power give you the ability to plant ideas into the world and see them grow. Naturally courageous, active and headstrong, you're ruled by the head and you lead with it. When you're thriving, you're easily the most lively and daring of all the signs, always on the lookout for new adventures, brimming with confidence and an innocent zest for life.

Your enormous energy and self-belief motivate those around you, while your drive and determination to succeed make you a natural leader, seldom held back by what others see as obstacles.

Of course, when you love being in charge, it can be difficult to take orders from others, but your warm heart and deep-seated sense of fair play make you a loyal ally, partner and friend. The slightest sense of injustice, and you're standing up for those you love.

Your independent spirit means you relish freedom, but this doesn't necessarily mean you like being alone. Upbeat and magnetic, you make a great friend. You like to party, and your sociable and energetic nature means you're up for anything.

Straightforward and honest, there's no fakery here – what you see is what you get. Able to take on many roles, you are the optimistic one when times get tough, inspiring those around you to tap into their potential, bringing out their best.

Likes

Being first
Getting lots of attention
Physical challenges
Coming up with original ideas
Being listened to

Dislikes

Being told what to do
Being overlooked or ignored
Having to wait

HOW TO BRING OUT YOUR BEST

For Aries, that eagerness to be first can mean you sometimes rush headlong into things, just like your animal sign, the ram, with little thought for the consequences. And searching for the next new and exciting thing might see you forget to finish what you started – do you tend to leave a trail of incomplete tasks and projects behind you?

Keep in mind that your boredom threshold is low, and when the challenge fades, so can your enthusiasm. You may switch from utterly obsessed to uninterested in an instant. Your impatient nature demands change, and you can become irritable and even angry if this need isn't met – you're a Fire sign, after all. Luckily that quick temper is usually short-lived, and you forgive just as fast.

You love to forge ahead, but it's worth taking the time to think how your actions might impact others. Why not use your competitive streak and challenge yourself to be more aware of others' feelings with each passing day?

Look for positive ways to use your many strengths – used in the wrong way, they can leave you struggling to be happy with who you really are.

Strengths

Courageous

Honest

Warm

Genuine

Independent

Fun

Weaknesses

Restless

Insensitive

Pushy

Selfish

Bad-tempered

SECRET FEARS

The downside of being such a naturally positive soul is when something doesn't go to plan. This can be a huge blow, and you will often blame yourself.

The same goes for arguments with friends. Deep down, you're worried about losing them. Your directness and feisty nature can push friends away – the day after an argument you've already moved on, but others can find it tricky to let things go so easily.

You have your friends' backs, and they can trust you to stand up for them and cheer them on. But inside you know you can't always depend on others to do the same for you, and your worries are often justified. You probably have a few stories about a time a supposed friend let you down.

· ·

Most likely to ...

Feel every emotion possible in the space of an hour

Kick something then get mad that it hurt

Get ready for school in two minutes flat

Tell someone you aren't angry, angrily

Be told to think before you act

Say: 'I was about to do that, but then you told me to'

Your RISING sign

YOUR RISING SIGN

Your Rising sign, also known as your Ascendant, is the sign that was rising over the Eastern horizon (the place where the Sun rises each day) when you were born. It describes how you see the world and the people around you and how they see you – the first impression that you give and receive, the image you project and the initial reaction you might have to a new situation. A person with Leo Rising, for example, may strike you as warm and engaging, whereas Pisces Rising is more sensitive and possibly shy. Because the Ascendant is determined by the exact time and place you were born, it is the most personal point in your chart. Many astrologers believe this makes it just as important as your Sun sign.

HOW TO FIND YOUR ASCENDANT

This is where it gets a bit tricky. There's a reason that popular astrology only deals with your Sun sign – your Rising sign can be more difficult to work out. But don't be put off. If you know your Sun sign and your time of birth, you can use the table on the right to give you a good idea. To be totally accurate you do need to take into account factors like time zone and daylight savings, and there are plenty of free online calculators that will do just that.

YOUR SUN SIGN	6:00 AM to 8:00 AM	8:00 AM to 10:00 AM	10:00 AM to 12:00 PM	12:00 PM to 2:00 PM	2:00 PM to 4:00 PM	4:00 PM to 6:00 PM	6:00 PM to 8:00 PM	8:00 PM to 10:00 PM	10:00 PM to 12:00 AM	12:00 AM to 2:00 AM	2:00 AM to 4:00 AM	4:00 AM to 6:00 AM
ARIES ♈	♉	♊	♋	♌	♍	♎	♏	♐	♑	♒	♓	♈
TAURUS ♉	♊	♋	♌	♍	♎	♏	♐	♑	♒	♓	♈	♉
GEMINI ♊	♋	♌	♍	♎	♏	♐	♑	♒	♓	♈	♉	♊
CANCER ♋	♌	♍	♎	♏	♐	♑	♒	♓	♈	♉	♊	♋
LEO ♌	♍	♎	♏	♐	♑	♒	♓	♈	♉	♊	♋	♌
VIRGO ♍	♎	♏	♐	♑	♒	♓	♈	♉	♊	♋	♌	♍
LIBRA ♎	♏	♐	♑	♒	♓	♈	♉	♊	♋	♌	♍	♎
SCORPIO ♏	♐	♑	♒	♓	♈	♉	♊	♋	♌	♍	♎	♏
SAGITTARIUS ♐	♑	♒	♓	♈	♉	♊	♋	♌	♍	♎	♏	♐
CAPRICORN ♑	♒	♓	♈	♉	♊	♋	♌	♍	♎	♏	♐	♑
AQUARIUS ♒	♓	♈	♉	♊	♋	♌	♍	♎	♏	♐	♑	♒
PISCES ♓	♈	♉	♊	♋	♌	♍	♎	♏	♐	♑	♒	♓

YOUR HOUR OF BIRTH

WHAT YOUR RISING SIGN SAYS ABOUT YOU

Once you have figured out your Ascendant, you are ready to discover more about how you see the world, and how it sees you.

ARIES RISING

Twice an Aries, the essence of your inner self matches the way you deal with others. This gives you a wonderfully straightforward approach – what you see is what you get. You are a force to be reckoned with, you champion those close to you and you act on your instincts. Brimming with ideas, your challenge is to stay the course – when the going gets tough, you have a strong tendency to change direction. Try to remember past failures and learn from them, or you are likely to make the same mistakes more than once.

TAURUS RISING

Careful and orderly, Taurus prefers a slower, more steady approach to life – very different to your Aries nature, which bubbles away under your calm exterior. You can seem stubborn and find it difficult to take advice – instead of imposing your views on others, try to use your creative talents to find solutions that work for everyone. Taurus also gives you a polite and sociable manner, which means you make friends easily. Looking good is important to you, and you probably know how to dress to impress.

GEMINI RISING

Your energy and motivation know no bounds. Gemini are great communicators, so make the most of this talent and look for causes that really inspire you and opportunities to convey messages you believe in. Remember, though, that everyone can benefit from talking a little less and listening more. Take a breath and wait for the right time before speaking. Bright, smart and easily bored, don't let a lack of focus keep you from reaching your dreams – find something that sparks your curiosity and stick with it.

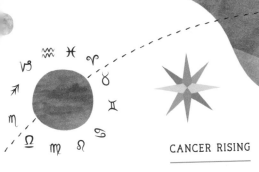

CANCER RISING

The meshing of these two very different signs can produce an intense desire to protect those you love. Your heart is in the right place, just don't forget to take a step back once in a while and ask yourself if they really need a knight in shining armour. Your need for security combined with your drive and ambition can mean you work too hard and find it difficult to switch off and relax. But your intuition, kindness and understanding of others will be a huge asset once you enter the workplace, and you will make the best kind of boss and colleague.

LEO RISING

Being admired by others is key when it comes to Leo, and this works in harmony with your positive outlook on life. Animated and laid-back, you express yourself with ease. You're happy to stand up, be counted and take the lead. You'll jump at the chance in class to head up a project, and what's more, you inspire other students to step up to the plate. Learning to be a follower at times – and smile while you're doing it – is one of your life challenges.

VIRGO RISING

Virgo has a talent for heading problems off at the pass, and partnered with your instinct to take the initiative, you're sure to be a whizz at solving things. You probably love a well-ordered list, too, and you project a self-assured, capable air. Sometimes, however, Virgo's influence can make you overthink situations and second-guess yourself. Have confidence that you're making the right choices, but also remember that everyone makes mistakes occasionally and it's okay to fail – that's how we grow and develop.

LIBRA RISING

Superb people skills are the gift of this pairing. Intelligent and charming, Libra also gives you an aura of poise and elegance that draws people to you. You were born to socialize, and have a real talent for helping friends get along and see each other's point of view. Although this also means you're the one most likely to be caught in the middle of your friends' arguments. You love to connect with others, and relationships will play a hugely important role in your life.

SCORPIO RISING

You can be a human whirlwind. Dynamic, intense and energetic, you are determined to be number one. Obstacles only make you more resolute – you refuse to give up. Scorpio does make sure you look before you leap into situations that may not be in your best interest, though. And slowing down a little may mean you get more done, simply because you're not juggling too many commitments at once.

SAGITTARIUS RISING

A sense of freedom is essential to you, and being cooped up inside can make you pretty miserable. This can be just as true for your relationships – you hate to feel trapped or pinned down. It's a different story when you're in the great outdoors, though, where you positively thrive. You're constantly on the go, bright and sociable, and you're deeply altruistic. You really care about those less lucky than yourself, and you spend time thinking about ways society could be improved.

CAPRICORN RISING

With this nimble-footed sign in your stars, you know how to watch your step, even when the going gets tough. When you set a goal – to reach the top of the class, perhaps – you devise a plan and then head purposefully towards it. Friends will admire your qualities of loyalty and determination – just try not to get so swallowed up in meeting targets that you run out of time to spend with them. In the working world, your rock-solid dependability will bring you to the attention of people who can really help to make your future career soar.

AQUARIUS RISING

Rebellious and idealistic, you are a maverick, and your talent for coming up with original ideas coupled with your ability to get projects off the ground can give you a real entrepreneurial streak. Determined to reach your goals, you push past obstacles with ease. You come across as open and interesting, which means you make friends effortlessly – your challenge is to spend time getting to know them on a deeper level, as you tend to lose interest quickly.

PISCES RISING

This combination isn't always a comfortable one. Your Pisces Ascendant gives you a dreamy appearance, and you come across as emotionally sensitive when in reality you're a whole lot tougher. When it comes to getting things done, you're often pulled in two different directions. Your inner Aries wants to take action, while your outer Pisces is more cautious. It's in your idealism that you feel most at ease. You strive for perfection and care deeply about making the world a better place.

Your MOON sign

YOUR MOON SIGN

The Moon rules your emotions and your inner moods, telling you what you need to feel safe, comfortable and loved. Knowing your Moon sign should give you a more complete picture of your unique self, helping you to express needs you might be struggling to understand. Suppose your Sun sign is Aries but being first has never been important to you – a Moon in Virgo may be telling you to hang back and fade into the background. Or you might have the Sun in home-loving Cancer but feel an urge to get out there and see the world. Perhaps that's because your Moon is in freedom-loving Sagittarius.

HOW TO FIND YOUR MOON SIGN

Just like your Rising sign, finding your Moon sign is more complicated than finding your Sun sign. That's because the Moon seems to move so quickly, taking just about a month to pass through all of the constellations. Thankfully, the tables on the right and on the next page make finding it a simple process.

First, find your year of birth. Then locate your birth month at the top of the table. Find your date of birth in the column below it, and this will give you your Moon sign. If your date of birth isn't listed, the one before it is your Moon sign.

For example, suppose your date of birth is 4 March, 1995. The date before this is 2 March, for which the Moon sign is Aries. This would mean your Moon sign is Aries.

BORN IN THE YEAR 1995

JAN	FEB	MAR	APR	MAY	JUN	JUL	AUG	SEP	OCT	NOV	DEC
2 Aqu	1 Pis	2 Ari	1 Tau	1 Gem	2 Leo	2 Vir	3 Sco	1 Sag	2 Aqu	1 Pis	3 Tau
4 Pis	3 Ari	5 Tau	3 Gem	3 Can	5 Vir	4 Lib	5 Sag	3 Cap	5 Pis	3 Ari	5 Gem
7 Ari	5 Tau	7 Gem	6 Can	6 Leo	7 Lib	6 Sco	7 Cap	5 Aqu	7 Ari	5 Tau	8 Can
9 Tau	8 Gem	10 Can	9 Leo	8 Vir	9 Sco	8 Sag	9 Aqu	7 Pis	9 Tau	8 Gem	10 Leo
12 Gem	10 Can	12 Leo	11 Vir	10 Lib	11 Sag	10 Cap	11 Pis	9 Ari	12 Gem	10 Can	13 Vir
14 Can	13 Leo	14 Vir	13 Lib	13 Sco	13 Cap	12 Aqu	13 Ari	12 Tau	14 Can	13 Leo	15 Lib
16 Leo	15 Vir	17 Lib	15 Sco	15 Sag	15 Aqu	14 Pis	15 Tau	14 Gem	17 Leo	15 Vir	17 Sco
19 Vir	17 Lib	19 Sco	17 Sag	17 Cap	17 Pis	17 Ari	18 Gem	17 Can	19 Vir	18 Lib	19 Sag
21 Lib	19 Sco	21 Sag	19 Cap	19 Aqu	19 Ari	19 Tau	20 Can	19 Leo	21 Lib	20 Sco	21 Cap
23 Sco	22 Sag	23 Cap	21 Aqu	21 Pis	22 Tau	22 Gem	23 Leo	22 Vir	23 Sco	22 Sag	23 Aqu
25 Sag	24 Cap	25 Aqu	24 Pis	23 Ari	24 Gem	24 Can	25 Vir	24 Lib	26 Sag	24 Cap	25 Pis
27 Cap	26 Aqu	27 Pis	26 Ari	26 Tau	27 Can	27 Leo	28 Lib	26 Sco	28 Cap	26 Aqu	28 Ari
30 Aqu	28 Pis	30 Ari	28 Tau	28 Gem	29 Leo	29 Vir	30 Sco	28 Sag	30 Aqu	28 Pis	30 Tau
				31 Can		31 Lib		30 Cap		30 Ari	

BORN IN THE YEAR 1996

JAN	FEB	MAR	APR	MAY	JUN	JUL	AUG	SEP	OCT	NOV	DEC
1 Gem	3 Leo	1 Leo	2 Lib	2 Sco	2 Cap	2 Aqu	2 Ari	1 Tau	3 Can	2 Leo	2 Vir
4 Can	5 Vir	3 Vir	4 Sco	4 Sag	4 Aqu	4 Pis	4 Tau	3 Gem	5 Leo	4 Vir	4 Lib
6 Leo	8 Lib	6 Lib	7 Sag	6 Cap	6 Pis	6 Ari	7 Gem	6 Can	8 Vir	7 Lib	6 Sco
9 Vir	10 Sco	8 Sco	9 Cap	8 Aqu	9 Ari	8 Tau	9 Can	8 Leo	10 Lib	9 Sco	9 Sag
11 Lib	12 Sag	10 Sag	11 Aqu	10 Pis	11 Tau	11 Gem	12 Leo	11 Vir	13 Sco	11 Sag	11 Cap
14 Sco	14 Cap	13 Cap	13 Pis	12 Ari	13 Gem	13 Can	14 Vir	13 Lib	15 Sag	13 Cap	13 Aqu
16 Sag	16 Aqu	15 Aqu	15 Ari	15 Tau	16 Can	16 Leo	17 Lib	15 Sco	17 Cap	16 Aqu	15 Pis
18 Cap	18 Pis	17 Pis	17 Tau	17 Gem	18 Leo	18 Vir	19 Sco	18 Sag	19 Aqu	18 Pis	17 Ari
20 Aqu	20 Ari	19 Ari	20 Gem	19 Can	21 Vir	21 Lib	21 Sag	20 Cap	21 Pis	20 Ari	19 Tau
22 Pis	23 Tau	21 Tau	22 Can	22 Leo	23 Lib	23 Sco	24 Cap	22 Aqu	23 Ari	22 Tau	22 Gem
24 Ari	25 Gem	23 Gem	25 Leo	25 Vir	26 Sco	25 Sag	26 Aqu	24 Pis	26 Tau	24 Gem	24 Can
26 Tau	27 Can	26 Can	27 Vir	27 Lib	28 Sag	27 Cap	28 Pis	26 Ari	28 Gem	27 Can	26 Leo
29 Gem		28 Leo	30 Lib	29 Sco	30 Cap	29 Aqu	30 Ari	28 Tau	30 Can	29 Leo	29 Vir
31 Can		31 Vir		31 Sag		31 Pis		30 Gem			31 Lib

BORN IN THE YEAR 1997

JAN	FEB	MAR	APR	MAY	JUN	JUL	AUG	SEP	OCT	NOV	DEC
3 Sco	1 Sag	1 Sag	1 Aqu	1 Pis	1 Tau	1 Gem	2 Leo	3 Lib	3 Sco	1 Sag	1 Cap
5 Sag	4 Cap	3 Cap	4 Pis	3 Ari	4 Gem	3 Can	4 Vir	6 Sco	5 Sag	4 Cap	3 Aqu
7 Cap	6 Aqu	5 Aqu	6 Ari	5 Tau	6 Can	5 Leo	7 Lib	8 Sag	8 Cap	6 Aqu	5 Pis
9 Aqu	8 Pis	7 Pis	8 Tau	7 Gem	8 Leo	8 Vir	9 Sco	10 Cap	10 Aqu	8 Pis	8 Ari
11 Pis	10 Ari	9 Ari	10 Gem	9 Can	11 Vir	10 Lib	12 Sag	12 Aqu	12 Pis	10 Ari	10 Tau
13 Ari	12 Tau	11 Tau	12 Can	12 Leo	13 Lib	13 Sco	14 Cap	15 Pis	14 Ari	12 Tau	12 Gem
15 Tau	14 Gem	13 Gem	14 Leo	14 Vir	16 Sco	15 Sag	16 Aqu	17 Ari	16 Tau	14 Gem	14 Can
18 Can	16 Can	16 Can	17 Vir	17 Lib	18 Sag	18 Cap	18 Pis	19 Tau	18 Gem	17 Can	16 Leo
20 Can	19 Leo	18 Leo	19 Lib	19 Sco	20 Cap	20 Aqu	20 Ari	21 Gem	20 Can	19 Leo	19 Vir
23 Leo	21 Vir	21 Vir	22 Sco	22 Sag	22 Aqu	22 Pis	22 Tau	23 Can	23 Leo	21 Vir	21 Lib
25 Vir	24 Lib	23 Lib	24 Sag	24 Cap	24 Pis	24 Ari	24 Gem	25 Leo	25 Vir	24 Lib	24 Sco
28 Lib	26 Sco	26 Sco	27 Cap	26 Aqu	26 Ari	26 Tau	27 Can	28 Vir	28 Lib	26 Sco	26 Sag
30 Sco		28 Sag	29 Aqu	28 Pis	29 Tau	28 Gem	29 Leo	30 Lib	30 Sco	29 Sag	28 Cap
		30 Cap		30 Ari		30 Can	31 Vir				31 Aqu

BORN IN THE YEAR 1998

JAN	FEB	MAR	APR	MAY	JUN	JUL	AUG	SEP	OCT	NOV	DEC
2 Pis	2 Tau	2 Tau	2 Can	2 Leo	3 Lib	3 Sco	2 Sag	3 Aqu	2 Pis	1 Ari	2 Gem
4 Ari	4 Gem	4 Gem	4 Leo	4 Vir	5 Sco	5 Sag	4 Cap	5 Pis	4 Ari	3 Tau	4 Can
6 Tau	7 Can	6 Can	7 Vir	7 Lib	8 Sag	8 Cap	6 Aqu	7 Ari	6 Tau	5 Gem	6 Leo
8 Gem	9 Leo	8 Leo	9 Lib	9 Sco	10 Cap	10 Aqu	8 Pis	9 Tau	8 Gem	7 Can	9 Vir
10 Can	11 Vir	11 Vir	12 Sco	12 Sag	13 Aqu	12 Pis	10 Ari	11 Gem	10 Can	9 Leo	11 Lib
13 Leo	14 Lib	13 Lib	14 Sag	14 Cap	15 Pis	14 Ari	13 Tau	13 Can	13 Leo	11 Vir	14 Sco
15 Vir	16 Sco	16 Sco	17 Cap	16 Aqu	17 Ari	16 Tau	15 Gem	15 Leo	15 Vir	14 Lib	16 Sag
18 Lib	19 Sag	18 Sag	19 Aqu	19 Pis	19 Tau	18 Gem	17 Can	18 Vir	17 Lib	16 Sco	19 Cap
20 Sco	21 Cap	21 Cap	21 Pis	21 Ari	21 Gem	21 Can	19 Leo	20 Lib	20 Sco	19 Sag	21 Aqu
23 Sag	23 Aqu	23 Aqu	23 Ari	23 Tau	23 Can	23 Leo	21 Vir	23 Sco	23 Sag	21 Cap	23 Pis
25 Cap	25 Pis	25 Pis	25 Tau	25 Gem	25 Leo	25 Vir	24 Lib	25 Sag	25 Cap	24 Aqu	25 Ari
27 Aqu	27 Ari	27 Ari	27 Gem	27 Can	28 Vir	28 Lib	26 Sco	28 Cap	27 Aqu	26 Pis	28 Tau
29 Pis		29 Tau	29 Can	29 Leo	30 Lib	30 Sco	29 Sag	30 Aqu	30 Pis	28 Ari	30 Gem
31 Ari		31 Gem		31 Vir			31 Cap			30 Tau	

JAN	FEB	MAR	APR	MAY	JUN	JUL	AUG	SEP	OCT	NOV	DEC

BORN IN THE YEAR 1999

JAN	FEB	MAR	APR	MAY	JUN	JUL	AUG	SEP	OCT	NOV	DEC
1 Can	1 Vir	1 Vir	2 Sco	2 Sag	3 Aqu	2 Pis	1 Ari	2 Gem	1 Can	1 Vir	1 Lib
3 Leo	4 Lib	3 Lib	4 Sag	4 Cap	5 Pis	5 Ari	3 Tau	4 Can	3 Leo	4 Lib	3 Sco
5 Vir	6 Sco	6 Sco	7 Cap	7 Aqu	8 Ari	7 Tau	5 Gem	6 Leo	5 Vir	6 Sco	6 Sag
7 Lib	9 Sag	8 Sag	9 Aqu	9 Pis	10 Tau	9 Gem	7 Can	8 Vir	8 Lib	9 Sag	8 Cap
10 Sco	11 Cap	11 Cap	12 Pis	11 Ari	12 Gem	11 Can	9 Leo	10 Lib	10 Sco	11 Cap	11 Aqu
12 Sag	14 Aqu	13 Aqu	14 Ari	13 Tau	14 Can	13 Leo	12 Vir	13 Sco	12 Sag	14 Aqu	13 Pis
15 Cap	16 Pis	15 Pis	16 Tau	15 Gem	16 Leo	15 Vir	14 Lib	15 Sag	15 Cap	16 Pis	16 Ari
17 Aqu	18 Ari	17 Ari	18 Gem	17 Can	18 Vir	17 Lib	16 Sco	18 Cap	17 Aqu	18 Ari	18 Tau
19 Pis	20 Tau	19 Tau	20 Can	19 Leo	20 Lib	20 Sco	19 Sag	20 Aqu	20 Pis	21 Tau	20 Gem
22 Ari	22 Gem	21 Gem	22 Leo	21 Vir	23 Sco	22 Sag	21 Cap	22 Pis	22 Ari	23 Gem	22 Can
24 Tau	24 Can	23 Can	24 Vir	24 Lib	25 Sag	25 Cap	24 Aqu	25 Ari	24 Tau	25 Can	24 Leo
26 Gem	26 Leo	26 Leo	27 Lib	26 Sco	28 Cap	27 Aqu	26 Pis	27 Tau	26 Gem	27 Leo	26 Vir
28 Can		28 Vir	29 Sco	29 Sag	30 Aqu	30 Pis	28 Ari	29 Gem	28 Can	29 Vir	28 Lib
30 Leo		30 Lib		31 Cap			30 Tau		30 Leo		31 Sco

BORN IN THE YEAR 2000

JAN	FEB	MAR	APR	MAY	JUN	JUL	AUG	SEP	OCT	NOV	DEC
3 Sag	1 Cap	2 Aqu	1 Pis	3 Tau	1 Gem	2 Leo	1 Vir	2 Sco	1 Sag	3 Aqu	2 Pis
5 Cap	4 Aqu	4 Pis	3 Ari	5 Gem	3 Can	4 Vir	3 Lib	4 Sag	4 Cap	5 Pis	4 Ari
7 Aqu	6 Pis	7 Ari	5 Tau	7 Can	5 Leo	7 Lib	5 Sco	6 Cap	6 Aqu	8 Ari	7 Tau
10 Pis	8 Ari	9 Tau	7 Gem	9 Leo	7 Vir	9 Sco	8 Sag	9 Aqu	9 Pis	10 Tau	9 Gem
12 Ari	11 Tau	11 Gem	9 Can	11 Vir	9 Lib	11 Sag	10 Cap	11 Pis	11 Ari	12 Gem	11 Can
14 Tau	13 Gem	13 Can	11 Leo	13 Lib	12 Sco	14 Cap	13 Aqu	14 Ari	13 Tau	14 Can	13 Leo
16 Gem	15 Can	15 Leo	14 Vir	15 Sco	14 Sag	16 Aqu	15 Pis	16 Tau	16 Gem	16 Leo	15 Vir
18 Can	17 Leo	17 Vir	16 Lib	18 Sag	17 Cap	19 Pis	18 Ari	18 Gem	18 Can	18 Vir	18 Lib
20 Leo	19 Vir	20 Lib	18 Sco	20 Cap	19 Aqu	21 Ari	20 Tau	20 Can	20 Leo	20 Lib	20 Sco
23 Vir	21 Lib	22 Sco	21 Sag	23 Aqu	22 Pis	24 Tau	22 Gem	23 Leo	22 Vir	23 Sco	22 Sag
25 Lib	23 Sco	24 Sag	23 Cap	25 Pis	24 Ari	26 Gem	24 Can	25 Vir	24 Lib	25 Sag	25 Cap
27 Sco	26 Sag	27 Cap	26 Aqu	28 Ari	26 Tau	28 Can	26 Leo	27 Lib	26 Sco	27 Cap	27 Aqu
29 Sag	28 Cap	29 Aqu	28 Pis	30 Tau	28 Gem	30 Leo	28 Vir	29 Sco	29 Sag	30 Aqu	30 Pis
			30 Ari		30 Can		30 Lib		31 Cap		

BORN IN THE YEAR 2001

JAN	FEB	MAR	APR	MAY	JUN	JUL	AUG	SEP	OCT	NOV	DEC
1 Ari	2 Gem	1 Gem	2 Leo	1 Vir	2 Sco	1 Sag	3 Agu	1 Pis	1 Ari	2 Gem	2 Can
4 Tau	4 Can	4 Can	4 Vir	3 Lib	4 Sag	4 Cap	5 Pis	4 Ari	4 Tau	4 Can	4 Leo
6 Gem	6 Leo	6 Leo	6 Lib	6 Sco	7 Cap	6 Aqu	8 Ari	6 Tau	6 Gem	7 Leo	6 Vir
8 Can	8 Vir	8 Vir	8 Sco	8 Sag	9 Aqu	9 Pis	10 Tau	8 Gem	8 Can	9 Vir	8 Lib
10 Leo	10 Lib	10 Lib	10 Sag	10 Cap	11 Pis	11 Ari	12 Gem	11 Can	10 Leo	11 Lib	10 Sco
12 Vir	12 Sco	12 Sco	13 Cap	13 Aqu	14 Ari	14 Tau	15 Can	13 Leo	13 Vir	13 Sco	12 Sag
14 Lib	15 Sag	14 Sag	15 Aqu	15 Pis	16 Tau	16 Gem	17 Leo	15 Vir	15 Lib	15 Sag	15 Cap
16 Sco	17 Cap	16 Cap	18 Pis	18 Ari	19 Gem	18 Can	19 Vir	17 Lib	17 Sco	17 Cap	17 Aqu
18 Sag	20 Agu	19 Aqu	20 Ari	20 Tau	21 Can	20 Leo	21 Lib	19 Sco	19 Sag	20 Aqu	20 Pis
21 Cap	22 Pis	22 Pis	23 Tau	22 Gem	23 Leo	22 Vir	23 Sco	21 Sag	21 Cap	22 Pis	22 Ari
23 Aqu	25 Ari	24 Ari	25 Gem	24 Can	25 Vir	24 Lib	25 Sag	24 Cap	23 Aqu	25 Ari	25 Tau
26 Pis	27 Tau	26 Tau	27 Can	27 Leo	27 Lib	26 Sco	27 Cap	26 Aqu	26 Pis	27 Tau	27 Gem
28 Ari		29 Gem	29 Leo	29 Vir	29 Sco	29 Sag	30 Aqu	29 Pis	28 Ari	30 Gem	29 Can
31 Tau		31 Can		31 Lib		31 Cap			31 Tau		31 Leo

BORN IN THE YEAR 2002

JAN	FEB	MAR	APR	MAY	JUN	JUL	AUG	SEP	OCT	NOV	DEC
2 Vir	1 Lib	2 Sco	1 Sag	2 Aqu	1 Pis	1 Ari	2 Gem	1 Can	1 Leo	1 Lib	1 Sco
4 Lib	3 Sco	4 Sag	3 Cap	5 Pis	4 Ari	4 Tau	5 Can	3 Leo	3 Vir	3 Sco	3 Sag
6 Sco	5 Sag	6 Cap	5 Aqu	7 Ari	6 Tau	6 Gem	7 Leo	5 Vir	5 Lib	5 Sag	5 Cap
9 Sag	7 Cap	9 Aqu	8 Pis	10 Tau	9 Gem	8 Can	9 Vir	7 Lib	7 Sco	7 Cap	7 Aqu
11 Cap	10 Aqu	11 Pis	10 Ari	12 Gem	11 Can	11 Leo	11 Lib	9 Sco	9 Sag	10 Aqu	9 Pis
13 Aqu	12 Pis	14 Ari	13 Tau	15 Can	13 Leo	13 Vir	13 Sco	12 Sag	12 Cap	12 Pis	12 Ari
16 Pis	15 Ari	16 Tau	15 Gem	17 Leo	15 Vir	15 Lib	15 Sag	14 Cap	13 Aqu	15 Ari	14 Tau
18 Ari	17 Tau	19 Gem	18 Can	19 Vir	18 Lib	17 Sco	18 Cap	16 Aqu	16 Pis	17 Tau	17 Gem
21 Tau	20 Gem	21 Can	20 Leo	21 Lib	20 Sco	19 Sag	20 Aqu	19 Pis	18 Ari	20 Gem	19 Can
23 Gem	22 Can	24 Leo	22 Vir	23 Sco	22 Sag	21 Cap	22 Pis	21 Ari	21 Tau	22 Can	22 Leo
26 Can	24 Leo	26 Vir	24 Lib	25 Sag	24 Cap	24 Aqu	25 Ari	24 Tau	23 Gem	24 Leo	24 Vir
28 Leo	26 Vir	28 Lib	26 Sco	28 Cap	26 Aqu	26 Pis	27 Tau	26 Gem	26 Can	27 Vir	26 Sco
30 Vir	28 Lib	30 Sco	28 Sag	30 Aqu	29 Pis	28 Ari	30 Gem	29 Can	28 Leo	29 Lib	28 Sco
			30 Cap			31 Tau			30 Vir		30 Sag

JAN	FEB	MAR	APR	MAY	JUN	JUL	AUG	SEP	OCT	NOV	DEC

BORN IN THE YEAR 2003

JAN	FEB	MAR	APR	MAY	JUN	JUL	AUG	SEP	OCT	NOV	DEC
1 Cap	2 Pis	1 Pis	3 Tau	2 Gem	1 Can	1 Leo	2 Sag	2 Sag	1 Cap	2 Pis	2 Ari
3 Aqu	5 Ari	4 Ari	5 Gem	5 Can	4 Leo	3 Vir	4 Sco	4 Cap	4 Aqu	5 Ari	4 Tau
6 Pis	7 Tau	6 Tau	8 Can	7 Leo	6 Vir	5 Lib	6 Sag	6 Aqu	6 Pis	7 Tau	7 Gem
8 Ari	10 Gem	9 Gem	10 Leo	10 Vir	8 Lib	7 Sco	8 Cap	9 Pis	8 Ari	10 Gem	9 Can
11 Tau	12 Can	11 Can	12 Vir	12 Lib	10 Sco	10 Sag	10 Aqu	11 Ari	11 Tau	12 Can	12 Leo
13 Gem	14 Leo	14 Leo	14 Lib	14 Sco	12 Sag	12 Cap	12 Pis	13 Tau	13 Gem	15 Leo	14 Vir
16 Can	16 Vir	16 Vir	16 Sco	16 Sag	14 Cap	14 Aqu	15 Ari	16 Gem	16 Can	17 Vir	16 Lib
18 Leo	18 Lib	18 Lib	18 Sag	18 Cap	16 Aqu	16 Pis	17 Tau	18 Can	18 Leo	19 Lib	19 Sco
20 Vir	20 Sco	20 Sco	20 Cap	20 Aqu	19 Pis	18 Ari	20 Gem	21 Leo	21 Vir	21 Sco	21 Sag
22 Lib	23 Sag	22 Sag	23 Aqu	22 Pis	21 Ari	21 Tau	22 Can	23 Vir	23 Lib	23 Sag	23 Cap
24 Sco	25 Cap	24 Cap	25 Pis	25 Ari	23 Tau	23 Gem	24 Leo	25 Lib	25 Sco	25 Cap	25 Aqu
26 Sag	27 Aqu	26 Aqu	27 Ari	27 Tau	26 Gem	26 Can	27 Vir	27 Sco	27 Sag	27 Aqu	27 Pis
29 Cap		29 Pis	30 Tau	30 Gem	28 Can	28 Leo	29 Lib	29 Sag	29 Cap	29 Pis	29 Ari
31 Aqu		31 Ari				30 Vir	31 Sco		31 Aqu		

BORN IN THE YEAR 2004

JAN	FEB	MAR	APR	MAY	JUN	JUL	AUG	SEP	OCT	NOV	DEC
1 Tau	2 Can	3 Leo	1 Vir	1 Lib	2 Sag	1 Cap	1 Pis	2 Tau	2 Gem	1 Can	1 Leo
3 Gem	4 Leo	5 Vir	4 Lib	3 Sco	4 Cap	3 Aqu	4 Ari	5 Gem	5 Can	3 Leo	3 Vir
6 Can	7 Vir	7 Lib	6 Sco	5 Sag	6 Aqu	5 Pis	6 Tau	7 Can	7 Leo	6 Vir	6 Lib
8 Leo	9 Lib	9 Sco	9 Sag	7 Cap	8 Pis	7 Ari	8 Gem	10 Leo	10 Vir	8 Lib	8 Sco
10 Vir	11 Sco	12 Sag	10 Cap	9 Aqu	10 Ari	9 Tau	11 Can	12 Vir	12 Lib	10 Sco	10 Sag
13 Lib	13 Sag	14 Cap	12 Aqu	11 Pis	12 Tau	12 Gem	13 Leo	14 Lib	14 Sco	13 Sag	12 Cap
15 Sco	15 Cap	16 Aqu	14 Pis	14 Ari	15 Gem	15 Can	16 Vir	17 Sco	16 Sag	15 Cap	14 Aqu
17 Sag	17 Aqu	18 Pis	16 Ari	16 Tau	17 Can	17 Leo	18 Lib	19 Sag	18 Cap	17 Aqu	16 Pis
19 Cap	20 Pis	20 Ari	19 Tau	19 Gem	20 Leo	20 Vir	20 Sco	21 Cap	20 Aqu	19 Pis	18 Ari
21 Aqu	22 Ari	23 Tau	21 Gem	21 Can	22 Vir	22 Lib	23 Sag	23 Aqu	23 Pis	21 Ari	21 Tau
23 Pis	24 Tau	25 Gem	24 Can	24 Leo	25 Lib	24 Sco	25 Cap	25 Pis	25 Ari	23 Tau	23 Gem
25 Ari	27 Gem	28 Can	26 Leo	26 Vir	27 Sco	26 Sag	27 Aqu	27 Ari	27 Tau	26 Gem	25 Can
28 Tau	29 Can	30 Leo	29 Vir	28 Lib	29 Sag	28 Cap	29 Pis	30 Tau	29 Gem	28 Can	28 Leo
30 Gem				31 Sco		30 Aqu	31 Ari				31 Vir

BORN IN THE YEAR 2005

JAN	FEB	MAR	APR	MAY	JUN	JUL	AUG	SEP	OCT	NOV	DEC
2 Lib	1 Sco	2 Sag	3 Aqu	2 Pis	2 Gem	2 Can	1 Can	2 Vir	2 Lib	1 Sco	2 Cap
4 Sco	3 Sag	4 Cap	5 Pis	4 Ari	5 Can	5 Leo	3 Leo	5 Lib	4 Sco	3 Sag	4 Aqu
6 Sag	5 Cap	6 Aqu	7 Ari	6 Tau	7 Leo	7 Vir	6 Vir	7 Sco	7 Sag	5 Cap	7 Pis
8 Cap	7 Aqu	8 Pis	9 Tau	9 Gem	10 Vir	10 Lib	8 Lib	9 Sag	9 Cap	7 Aqu	9 Ari
10 Aqu	9 Pis	10 Ari	11 Gem	11 Can	12 Lib	12 Sco	11 Sco	12 Cap	11 Aqu	9 Pis	11 Tau
12 Pis	11 Ari	13 Tau	14 Can	14 Leo	15 Sco	15 Sag	13 Sag	14 Aqu	13 Pis	11 Ari	13 Gem
15 Ari	13 Tau	15 Gem	16 Leo	16 Vir	17 Sag	17 Cap	15 Cap	16 Pis	15 Ari	14 Tau	15 Can
17 Tau	16 Gem	17 Can	19 Vir	18 Lib	19 Cap	19 Aqu	17 Aqu	18 Ari	17 Tau	16 Gem	18 Leo
19 Gem	18 Can	20 Leo	21 Lib	21 Sco	21 Aqu	21 Pis	19 Pis	20 Tau	19 Gem	18 Can	20 Vir
22 Can	21 Leo	22 Vir	23 Sco	23 Sag	23 Pis	23 Ari	21 Ari	22 Gem	22 Can	21 Leo	23 Lib
24 Leo	23 Vir	25 Lib	26 Sag	25 Cap	25 Ari	25 Tau	23 Tau	24 Can	24 Leo	23 Vir	25 Sco
27 Vir	25 Lib	27 Sco	28 Cap	27 Aqu	28 Tau	27 Gem	26 Gem	27 Leo	27 Vir	26 Lib	28 Sag
29 Lib	28 Sco	29 Sag	30 Aqu	29 Pis	30 Gem	30 Can	28 Can	29 Vir	29 Lib	28 Sco	30 Cap
		31 Cap		31 Ari			31 Leo			30 Sag	

BORN IN THE YEAR 2006

JAN	FEB	MAR	APR	MAY	JUN	JUL	AUG	SEP	OCT	NOV	DEC
1 Aqu	1 Ari	1 Ari	1 Gem	1 Can	2 Vir	2 Lib	1 Sco	2 Cap	1 Aqu	2 Ari	1 Tau
3 Pis	3 Tau	3 Tau	4 Can	3 Leo	4 Lib	5 Sco	5 Sag	4 Aqu	4 Pis	4 Tau	3 Gem
5 Ari	6 Gem	5 Gem	6 Leo	6 Vir	7 Sco	7 Sag	6 Cap	6 Pis	6 Ari	6 Gem	6 Can
7 Tau	8 Can	7 Can	9 Vir	8 Lib	9 Sag	9 Cap	8 Aqu	8 Ari	8 Tau	8 Can	8 Leo
9 Gem	10 Leo	10 Leo	11 Lib	11 Sco	12 Cap	11 Aqu	10 Pis	10 Tau	10 Gem	10 Leo	10 Vir
12 Can	13 Vir	12 Vir	14 Sco	13 Sag	14 Aqu	13 Pis	12 Ari	12 Gem	12 Can	13 Vir	13 Lib
14 Leo	16 Lib	15 Lib	16 Sag	15 Cap	16 Pis	15 Ari	14 Tau	14 Can	14 Leo	15 Lib	15 Sco
17 Vir	18 Sco	17 Sco	18 Cap	18 Aqu	18 Ari	17 Tau	16 Gem	17 Leo	17 Vir	18 Sco	18 Sag
19 Lib	20 Sag	20 Sag	20 Aqu	20 Pis	20 Tau	20 Gem	18 Can	19 Vir	19 Lib	20 Sag	20 Cap
22 Sco	23 Cap	22 Cap	22 Pis	22 Ari	22 Gem	22 Can	21 Leo	22 Lib	22 Sco	23 Cap	22 Aqu
24 Sag	25 Aqu	24 Aqu	25 Ari	24 Tau	25 Can	24 Leo	23 Vir	24 Sco	24 Sag	25 Aqu	24 Pis
26 Cap	27 Pis	26 Pis	27 Tau	26 Gem	27 Leo	27 Vir	26 Lib	27 Sag	26 Cap	27 Pis	27 Ari
28 Aqu		28 Ari	29 Gem	28 Can	29 Vir	29 Lib	28 Sco	29 Cap	29 Aqu	29 Ari	29 Tau
30 Pis		30 Tau		31 Leo			31 Sag		31 Pis		31 Gem

WHAT YOUR MOON SIGN SAYS ABOUT YOU

Now that you know your Moon sign, read on to learn more about your emotional nature and your basic inner needs.

MOON IN ARIES

You have an emotional need to be first. And you want to be first *now* – there's no time to waste. Brimming with enthusiasm and energy, you love to keep busy and find waiting difficult. Remember to open up and talk to those closest to you about your feelings – they can help you to slow down and deal with any difficult emotions as they arise.

MOON IN TAURUS

You love to be surrounded by beautiful possessions and enjoy food and clothes that make you feel good – you have a need for comfort. Familiarity and routine are important to you, and you don't deal well with sudden change. That stubborn streak means you're able to stand up for yourself and protect your own interests, just remember to relax once in a while and try new things.

MOON IN GEMINI

Self-expression is one of your driving forces with this mix. Talking, drawing, writing – you simply have to communicate your feelings. And you love to listen to other peoples' ideas, too. To feed your curious intellect, you've probably got a tower of books and magazines at your bedside. Just don't forget to exercise your body as well as your mind.

MOON IN CANCER

You were born to nurture others – whether that's through baking them a cake or being at the end of the phone when they need your reassuring words. Family is hugely important to you, and you want to feel loved and secure. Being honest about this and accepting your wonderfully sensitive and emotional nature will help you find inner peace.

MOON IN LEO

You have an emotional need to be admired – all you really want is for everyone to love you. Your kind heart and generosity towards your friends and family means you are usually surrounded by others, and the attention you crave is easily won. When things don't go your way, you have a tendency to be dramatic – don't let your pride stop you from asking for help when you need it.

MOON IN VIRGO

You are a gentle soul and appreciate the simple things in life. Helping others in small ways makes you feel needed, secure and purposeful. A clean and tidy environment is a must, and everything has to be in its proper place. Learning not to fuss when something isn't perfect is a challenge – look for useful ways to keep your practical nature busy and happiness will follow.

MOON IN LIBRA

Close bonds are everything to you – you find strength and stability in your relationships with others. Your need for balance and harmony means you are an excellent peacemaker, skilled at helping people to see and understand another's perspective. Remember to feed your love of beauty with regular trips to art galleries and picturesque places.

MOON IN SCORPIO

Deep and emotionally intense, you need to trust those close to you with your innermost thoughts and desires. All or nothing, you have incredible intuition and can see right to the heart of people. Finding one or two close friends who you can really open up to and be honest with about your feelings is important for your happiness. When this happens, your inner strength is unmatched.

MOON IN SAGITTARIUS

Your need for freedom and space is overwhelming, but when you achieve it, you are bright, breezy and filled with a zest for life. Always on the lookout for new things to try and people to meet, your energy and enthusiasm lifts the spirits of those around you. Planning is not your strong suit; you prefer to go with the flow and see where it takes you – preferably somewhere fun and interesting!

MOON IN CAPRICORN

Ambitious and practical, you want to work hard and achieve results. You are conscientious and naturally organized, with a clear picture of what you want and how you intend to get there. Remember to take time to kick back and relax – the strong front you present to those around you can hide your more sensitive side. Letting go occasionally isn't a sign of weakness.

MOON IN AQUARIUS

Your desire to be unique and unusual is powerful, and you need the space and freedom to be yourself. Emotionally detached, you are happily independent and have an ability to see the bigger picture. Try not to lose touch with those closest to you – life is full of ups and downs, and friends and family can offer valuable support through tougher times.

MOON IN PISCES

Dreamy and intuitive, your sensitive nature is highly attuned to the feelings of others. Be careful to steer clear of negative people – you're likely to absorb their vibes, and they will bring you down. It's important you learn how to take care of yourself when you feel overwhelmed emotionally. Escaping into a good book or listening to your favourite music can be a great way to re-set.

ELEMENTS

YOUR ELEMENTAL TYPE

Fire, Earth, Air, Water – in ancient times these were thought to contain everything that existed on Earth. Today that's no longer the case, but there's no denying their powerful effect on people's lives. Think of the heat from the Sun, the way earth is used to grow food, the water you consume, the air that you breathe. And like so much in astrology, each element has two sides. You drink water and rain helps plants to grow, but the force of a tsunami can wreak havoc and destruction. You have all four elements within you, but one or more of them will stand out. You could be a single type, or a mix of two or three. Your elemental type says a lot about you and those you interact with. When you meet someone you feel naturally comfortable with, it's often because you are elementally compatible.

IN YOUR ELEMENT

As the hottest of the Fire signs, Aries, you are full of warmth, passion and energy. Like fireworks, which can be dramatic and unpredictable, you have a tendency to be spontaneous and impulsive. If you can control your dominant, fiery nature and learn to slow down when necessary, your natural self-confidence and love of life can be a huge inspiration to others.

 FIRE WITH FIRE

You get along well with other Fire signs, just as Earth will with Earth, and so on. Relationships are led by the heart rather than by the head, as you both love others freely and with your whole being. When arguments arise, sparks can fly. Cool off with a walk or some kind of physical activity.

 FIRE WITH EARTH

Not ideally compatible, as Earth extinguishes Fire, while 'scorched Earth' is sterile and unproductive. Still, Earth can slow you down, acting as a grounding force, while you might get them going, energizing them with your passion and intensity. Finding a balance between stability and some form of newness and excitement is essential to a happy relationship.

 FIRE WITH AIR

Fire and Air signs are wonderfully compatible – think of oxygen to a flame. Air is full of ideas, and you are ready to put them into action. Together, you are a powerful, unstoppable force of activity. Remember, though, that relationships can become overwhelming if boundaries aren't put in place – Air has the ability to fuel Fire, but it can also blow it out.

 FIRE WITH WATER

Not an ideal mix. Fire and Water can be beautiful together, adventurous and dynamic, but if one is too dominant it can dampen Fire's energy or scorch Water's emotions. When it works, Water will bring sensitivity and comfort, while you provide motivation and the courage to act.

THE MISSING PIECE

How dominant Fire is within you depends on the influence of the other elements in your chart – ideally all four would be represented. Sometimes a lack of a particular element can cause an imbalance, making you feel rundown or stressed. The best way to counteract this is to tune in to the missing element and reharmonize yourself. Try the simple exercise below to get back in touch with any elements you're missing.

1. First, take a look at the Zodiac signs and their elements.

Fire: Aries, Leo, Sagittarius

Earth: Taurus, Virgo, Capricorn

Air: Gemini, Libra, Aquarius

Water: Cancer, Scorpio, Pisces

2. Now circle Fire, as this is the element that represents your Sun sign. You're certain to have some of this element. Then do the same for your Moon sign and your Ascendant, circling the element associated with each.

3. Looking at the list, there should be one or more elements you haven't circled.

Earth – a lack of Earth can make you feel disorganized, off-balance or like you couldn't care less. You might want more routine, structure or to stay focused.

Air – Air will help you to communicate better, feel more sociable and lift your spirits. Use it to boost your curiosity and sharpen your wits.

Water – with Water missing, you may struggle to get in touch with your emotions or worry you're being insensitive. You're looking to express yourself, to feel more creative and inspired.

4. Choose the element you would like to tune in to. Then pick one of the ideas from the lists below. If Earth is missing, you could take a picnic to the park and sit on the grass. If it's Water, you could try a soak in the bath. You can use this exercise whenever you feel out of balance.

EARTH

Grow tomatoes
Pick wildflowers
Collect stones
Camp in the garden
Do cartwheels on the grass
Build a sandcastle
Roll down a hill

AIR

Fly a kite
Watch clouds go by
Blow bubbles
Feel the breeze
Breathe deep
Play with a balloon
Chase butterflies

WATER

Spend a day at the beach
Splash in a puddle
Sit by a fountain
Walk in the rain
Catch a wave
Snorkel

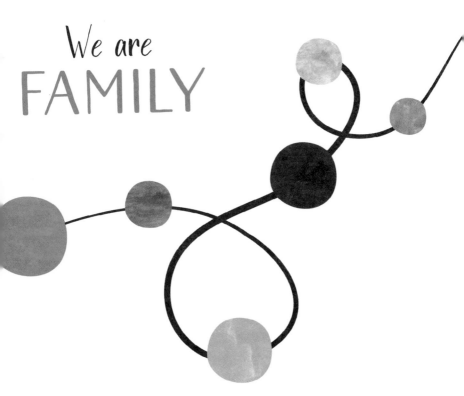

We are
FAMILY

WE'RE ALL IN THIS TOGETHER

When so much in your life is changing, your relationships with your parents can become even more important. If you're lucky, you get on well with yours, but even the most harmonious relationships can come under strain during the teenage years. How can astrology help? It can remind you that parents are people, too. They might not get everything right, but hopefully you believe that they have your best interests at heart. Learning more about who they are, why they do things and how you relate to them can make it easier for all of you to move forwards together.

MOTHER MOON

The Moon sign you are born with can tell you a lot about how you see and treat your mother. This is because your Moon sign represents your emotional needs – what you need to feel safe and secure – and these are most often fulfilled by your mother. How you react to her can make a big difference to the way she behaves around you. If you are visibly upset by certain things she does, she is likely to change her behaviour the next time around. If you react with happiness and delight, she is more likely to repeat them.

Here's how you see your mother according to your Moon sign...

ARIES

You view your mother as strong, honest and forthright. Sometimes, especially when she doesn't agree with your plans, this can make you feel as though she's taking over. Try not to push back too strongly, and remember she has your interests at heart.

TAURUS

You like to feel your mother is looking after all of your everyday needs and is dependable and reliable. Don't judge her too harshly if she doesn't always live up to your expectations – providing for others is often a careful balancing act, and she is likely doing her best.

GEMINI

Flighty and impulsive, you need your mother to give you the freedom to be yourself and make your own mistakes. Space and independence often have to be earned, though – what could you do to show her that you're capable and trustworthy?

CANCER

Your longing for your mother's emotional attention can give you a wonderful bond and connection. However, the slightest hint of rejection from her can wound you deeply. Try not to take her reactions personally – it's okay for her to make choices and have goals that differ from yours.

LEO

You want to enjoy an open, honest relationship with your mother, where both of you say what you mean. Underlying this candour is a need for assurance and acceptance – when you feel vulnerable, be brave and explain to her how you feel.

VIRGO

You are aware of who gives what in your emotional relationship with your mother, and occasionally this can make you feel that she isn't there for you. Viewing her actions as 'different' rather than 'wrong' will help you to trust she is doing what she thinks is right.

LIBRA

You need your mother to recognize your emotional needs as valid and important. Try not to spend too much time putting others first – your relationship will flourish when you both accept the roles you play.

SCORPIO

You want your mother to respect your emotional boundaries and allow you alone-time when you need it. The trust between you can be intense and unconditional, so much so you may have to remind her to step back occasionally.

SAGITTARIUS

Upbeat and curious, your relationship works best when your mother is inspiring and encouraging, giving you the emotional freedom you need to expand your horizons. It's fine to chase independence, as long as you respect your mother's desire to give you roots.

CAPRICORN

You empathize strongly with your mother's feelings, so when she's struggling, this can make you feel it's your fault. Learn to let go of this guilt – it's unintentional and unhelpful. Instead, recognize how much you need each other's emotional support and encouragement.

AQUARIUS

You're not sure your mother's attempts to guide you are always necessary, and don't like to burden her with your problems. Asking for help and talking things through might be more useful than you imagine and can bring you closer together at the same time.

PISCES

Your mother's high expectations have made you stronger emotionally, even though there are times when you just want to feel like a child and let her take care of everything. Taking responsibility can be tough; don't be afraid to speak up when you need support.

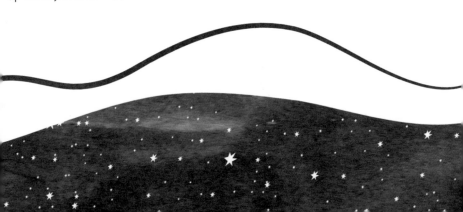

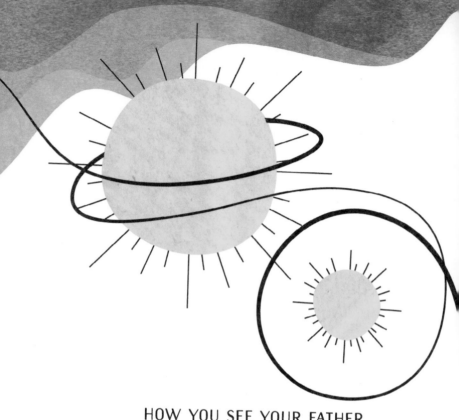

HOW YOU SEE YOUR FATHER

Just as your Moon sign gives you an indication of how you see your mother, or whoever plays that nurturing role in your life, your Sun sign can reveal the way you view your father, or the caregiver who is most involved with discipline. Your relationship with this person is built over time. For girls, it can have a strong bearing on how you view any future romantic relationships, whereas boys will either rebel or identify with these traits.

With your Aries Sun sign, you view your father as busy and always on the go. You feel he can be too quick to become impatient with you, and has trouble holding his temper. Showing interest in some of his favourite hobbies or activities can be a great way to bond and gain his attention.

Now read on to find out how your father's Sun sign affects your relationship . . .

Your father's Sun sign will play a significant part in how you relate to him, and it can help you to understand why he acts the way he does – however infuriating it may sometimes seem!

ARIES

You both like to be the one in charge, and this can lead to clashes. Slowing down and spending time one-on-one will benefit you both. Remember that winning a fight doesn't matter as much as what you can learn from it.

TAURUS

You like to push the boundaries and that's okay with your father. He knows it's important for you to explore your gifts and abilities. There's a lot of trust between the two of you because you can talk about pretty much anything.

GEMINI

This relationship is action-packed, and you'll enjoy hiking or cycling together. You both can lose interest in something quite quickly, dashing off towards the next thing. This means you can leave projects unfinished – but the high fun factor between you is what counts.

CANCER

Your high-energy approach to life might exhaust your dad on occasion. However, your home is filled with love and you will share one of life's most important lessons – how to respect and care about other people's feelings.

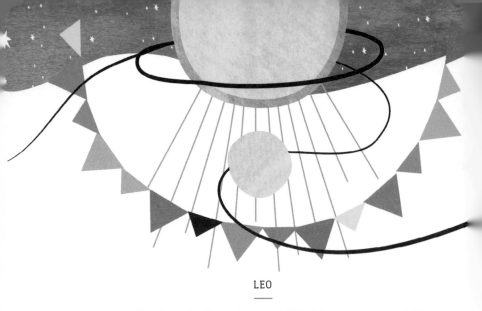

LEO

Your sisters and brothers don't need to watch TV with you two around. Your sparky relationship – both of you are pretty strong-willed – is entertainment enough! Luckily, you know when to pull back, so there's rarely any real upset.

VIRGO

With your fiery nature, you may sometimes push your father just to get an emotional reaction. Equally, he will teach you how to be patient and kind. And over time, the two of you will find a happy balance in your relationship.

LIBRA

Plans change in a heartbeat in this household, due to your dad's indecisive nature. It can drive you mad, but look at it another way: there's never a dull moment, is there? As opposite signs of the Zodiac, quarrels are inevitable, but they blow over quickly.

SCORPIO

You love each other fiercely, but the struggle is real. It's irrelevant what you clash over: it's all about the winning between you two. In time you will both develop a deep respect for each other and see the funny side of your animated relationship.

SAGITTARIUS

A shared love of make-believe and fantasy gives you a super-special bond. Even as you get older, you'll still (secretly) love to have your father read your favourite story to you. And happily, this level of communication will continue throughout your life.

CAPRICORN

You may feel that your dad puts the pressure on, but it's coming from a good place. He wants to see you soar, and this is his way of getting you there. And when you feel frustrated, remember that he's on your side.

AQUARIUS

There's a definite push and pull in this relationship. You want everything now, and your father is always thinking of the long game. Luckily, your shared view of the world at large helps to bridge the gap.

PISCES

Your dad knows that beneath the outgoing, bubbly face you show to the world there is a soft vulnerability. He encourages you to follow your dreams but will shower you with love when things don't go to plan.

Best of
FRIENDS

FRIENDS FOR LIFE

Friends play an essential role in your happiness. They can help you to move forwards when times are tough, see things from a new perspective and encourage you just to have fun. Every good friend you make has different qualities that will influence you and allow you to make more of your potential. A friend might show you it can be better to hold back when all you want to do is rush in, motivate you to stick with that project right to the end or inspire you to see an obstacle as a challenge. And astrology can be a great way to highlight those characteristics you're looking for in a friend. It can also tell you more about the type of friend you make for others.

WHAT KIND OF FRIEND ARE YOU?

As an Aries, you make friends easily. You are willing to help your friends achieve their goals, you see the best in them and are happy to take risks for them, too. You love to be someone's best friend and can find it difficult to feel second to anyone else. You are always on the lookout for new, super-fun adventures and are happy to take your friends along for the ride. You have a knack of bringing people from all walks of life together.

Strengths: *Loyal, generous, fun-loving*
Weaknesses: *Insensitive, demanding, petulant*
Friendship style: *Busy, fun, warm*

IF YOUR BEST FRIEND IS . . .

TAURUS

Considerate and charming, Taurus friends often have a talent for giving good advice. They like to take their time and allow friendships to develop slowly, but once you become close they treat you as a member of their family. As an Earth sign, they are dependable and grounded, and they make wonderful lifelong friends. Bear in mind they can place too much importance on material possessions, even judging others based on their wealth.

Strengths: *Caring, faithful, trustworthy*
Weaknesses: *Judgmental, stubborn, materialistic*
Friendship style: *Helpful, sweet, self-assured*

GEMINI

You'll need lots of energy to keep up with a Gemini friend. They love to have fun, do crazy things and always have a story to tell. They'll make you laugh, but they can sometimes get a little carried away, perhaps exaggerating tales of their adventures in their effort to entertain you. They can be a bit gossipy, but they're not malicious. They're good listeners and will make you feel great, giving you lots of compliments – and always genuine ones, too.

Strengths: *Intelligent, energetic, fearless*
Weaknesses: *Impatient, easily bored, gossipy*
Friendship style: *Good listener, witty, spontaneous*

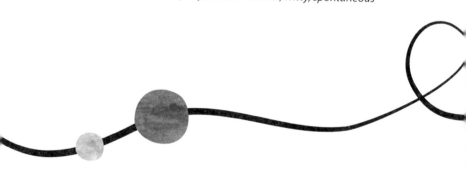

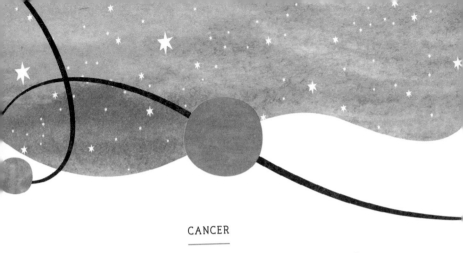

CANCER

Once you form a close connection with Cancer, you have a friend who has your back. They're considerate and like nothing better than to make you feel happy. Watch out though; they're deeply emotional, which means that if you argue – even over something small – you'll have to work hard to patch things up again.

Strengths: *Loving, caring, intuitive*
Weaknesses: *Unforgiving, anxious, sensitive*
Friendship style: *Warm, affectionate, protective*

LEO

As long as you don't expect too much from a Leo friend, you're in for a treat. Outgoing, confident and full of energy, they thrive on social occasions and love to be the life and soul of a party, making people laugh and being admired. They're good at bringing people together and are in high demand, so you won't always have them to yourself, but if you can tie them down you'll have some great quality one-on-one time.

Strengths: *Honest, brave, positive*
Weaknesses: *Arrogant, self-centred, proud*
Friendship style: *Supportive, cheerful, engaging*

VIRGO

With a Virgo by your side you'll always have somewhere to go when times are tough. They'll be there for you, giving you well-thought-out advice and a gentle sympathetic ear. Even when there's not a crisis, they're charming and kind. They like to be organized, so if they make plans, make sure you stick to them. They won't let you down, but they'll expect the same from you in return.

Strengths: *Warm, modest, smart*
Weaknesses: *Shy, serious, overly critical*
Friendship style: *Fixer, good communicator, reliable*

LIBRA

You can rely on your Libra friend to tell you how it is. They have a refreshing honesty, but they also have a diplomatic way of sparing your feelings. They love spending time with you and like nothing better than a chat (especially if they're the one doing the talking!). They can always see both sides, so if there's a disagreement it won't be for long.

Strengths: *Diplomatic, honest, sociable*
Weaknesses: *Indecisive, people pleaser, chatterbox*
Friendship style: *Laid-back, devoted, forgiving*

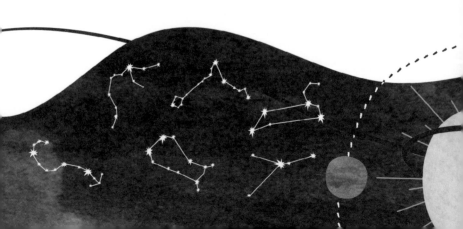

SCORPIO

It's an honour to be a Scorpio's best friend. They're selective, so they don't always have many, but the friendships they do make will be really special. Once you've cemented your friendship, they'll open their inner circle to you and will want to spend lots of time together. In return, they'll expect 100 per cent loyalty and might not take it well if you let them down, so tread carefully.

Strengths: *Passionate, hospitable, perceptive*
Weaknesses: *Guarded, jealous, suspicious*
Friendship style: *Intense, selective, loyal*

SAGITTARIUS

Sagittarius are low-maintenance friends. Easy-going, positive and happy-go-lucky, they're up for anything. If you fancy an adventure, give them a call, but don't expect too much of them feelings-wise. Their friendship circle is wide and diverse, so you'll get to meet lots of interesting people, but they are easily bored and can struggle with emotional closeness. On the plus side, they won't put too many demands on you, so give them some space and enjoy the ride.

Strengths: *Adventurous, positive, open-minded*
Weaknesses: *Impatient, insensitive, easily bored*
Friendship style: *Generous, undemanding, never dull*

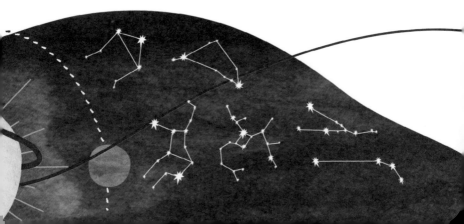

CAPRICORN

You might have to put in some groundwork but once you've cracked the seemingly aloof exterior of a Capricorn you'll have yourself a genuine, warm, loving and faithful friend. They'll show you complete devotion, through the good times and the bad. They're thoughtful and sensible, and will know when to call it a night, but they will often surprise you with their sly sense of humour. They love to make you smile.

Strengths: *Responsible, supportive, faithful*
Weaknesses: *Condescending, standoffish, serious*
Friendship style: *Thoughtful, rational, work hard/play hard*

AQUARIUS

You'll have to share your Aquarius best friend – they'll probably flit in and out of lots of other friendships, too – but rest assured they've got your back and will go to the ends of the Earth for you. They'll bring plenty of excitement and fun into your world, but they also treasure their alone time, so don't put too many demands on them. They'll never pass judgment on you, no matter what you do.

Strengths: *Tolerant, independent, energetic*
Weaknesses: *Easily bored, rebellious, forgetful*
Friendship style: *Fun, exciting, unpredictable*

PISCES

A Pisces friend is a great listener who is sympathetic and caring and will always make time for you. They're the perfect friend if you need a shoulder to cry on, but they can sometimes get too emotionally involved. If there is any discord in your friendship, they are quick to blame themselves. Reassure them and let them know it's not their fault and you'll soon win back their love and support.

Strengths: *Loving, caring, good listener*
Weaknesses: *Sensitive, self-pitying, insecure*
Friendship style: *Supportive, sympathetic, selfless*

Your BIRTHDAY log

List the birthdays of your family and friends and discover their Sun signs

ARIES

March 21–April 20

Passionate, energetic, impulsive

TAURUS

April 21–May 21

Steady, tenacious, trustworthy

GEMINI

May 22–June 21

Intelligent, outgoing, witty

CANCER

June 22–July 22

Caring, home-loving, affectionate

LEO

July 23–August 23

Loud, big-hearted, fun

VIRGO

Organized, modest, responsible

LIBRA

September 23–October 22

Charming, creative, graceful

SCORPIO

October 23–November 21

Powerful, mysterious, magnetic

SAGITTARIUS

November 22–December 21

Adventurous, optimistic, lucky

CAPRICORN

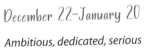

December 22–January 20

Ambitious, dedicated, serious

AQUARIUS

January 21–February 19

Eccentric, independent, imaginative

PISCES

February 20–March 20

Dreamy, sensitive, compassionate

Lucky in
LOVE

WHY OPPOSITES REALLY DO ATTRACT

The sign opposite your Ascendant (your Rising sign) on your birth chart reveals who you will attract, and who will attract you. Known as your Descendant, it's the constellation that was setting on the Western horizon at the moment and place you were born.

This sign is everything you are not – a kind of mirror image, or two sides of the same coin.

Yet, strangely, you are often drawn to the qualities of this sign over and over again in the people you meet. It's possible that these characteristics are ones you feel you lack yourself, and you sense that the other person can fill in what's missing. Sometimes it really is true that opposites attract!

Ascendant		Descendant
Aries		Libra
Taurus		Scorpio
Gemini		Sagittarius
Cancer		Capricorn
Leo		Aquarius
Virgo		Pisces
Libra		Aries
Scorpio		Taurus
Sagittarius		Gemini
Capricorn		Cancer
Aquarius		Leo
Pisces		Virgo

WHAT DO YOU LOOK FOR?

Once you've matched up your Ascendant with your Descendant from the list on page 81, you can get to know the qualities that are most likely to attract you. You can use this information whether you're thinking about romance or friendship.

LIBRA DESCENDANT

You're looking for balance and harmony in your relationship, with someone who makes you feel interesting and important. You want to be listened to, and value the ability to compromise. Gentleness and sensitivity are the qualities you're searching for.

SCORPIO DESCENDANT

You want an intense, passionate relationship with someone who will welcome you wholeheartedly into their world and want to spend lots of time with you. You are attracted to someone who will take control, but who will also look out for you and protect you.

SAGITTARIUS DESCENDANT

Adventure and fun are what you crave when it comes to love. You want someone open-minded who will accept you for who you are. You need to be given plenty of space to breathe and not be stifled by too many demands.

CAPRICORN DESCENDANT

You seek total dedication and devotion from those you love. You're happy to take your time and let a relationship develop naturally, and aren't put off by someone who appears cool or guarded. You like a cheeky sense of humour, too.

AQUARIUS DESCENDANT

You are attracted to someone who is independent and has a full life outside of your relationship, although you want to know that if push comes to shove, they will be right there for you. You like to be kept on your toes.

PISCES DESCENDANT

You're not afraid of a deep relationship with someone who wears their heart on their sleeve. You want to be cared for, emotionally supported and loved unconditionally. You want to be the centre of someone's world.

ARIES DESCENDANT

You like someone to spar with and who lets you have your own way, but is still strong enough to put their foot down when the gravity of the situation demands it. You will need to respect your partner's strength, bravery and integrity.

TAURUS DESCENDANT

Stability and reliability are high on your list of priorities when it comes to forming relationships. You dislike chaos and are drawn to people who you know won't surprise or disappoint you. Instead you want a partnership that's grounded and safe.

GEMINI DESCENDANT

You're attracted to someone who is spontaneous and fearless, and who can keep you entertained. You're likely to fall for someone who makes you feel super-special and is quick to recognize your achievements and boost your confidence.

CANCER DESCENDANT

You seek relationships where you're made to feel like one of the family, where your every need and demand is met, particularly emotionally. You want to feel warm and fuzzy and protected by those you love.

LEO DESCENDANT

You're drawn to someone who is strong, confident and outgoing with a busy social life but who can also give you warmth and passion when required. You're attracted to those who can make you laugh and sweep you off your feet.

VIRGO DESCENDANT

You long for kindness and tenderness in a partnership, along with reliability. You want someone who can bring order into your life and who will think things through in a methodical way. Nothing should be left to chance.

Life at
SCHOOL

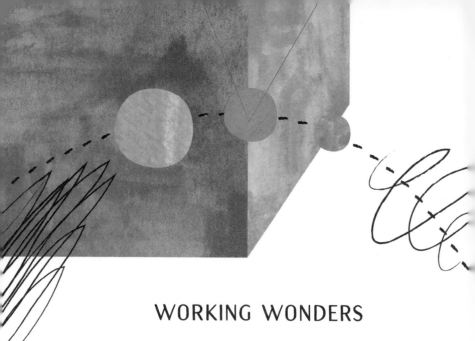

WORKING WONDERS

Have you ever been told that your years at school will be 'the best of your life'? Do you think they will be? Why? Many different things will determine how much you enjoy your school days. And there are sure to be ups and downs along the way. But there are a couple of important factors that astrology can help with. The first is determining your skills and strengths, and the second is learning to work well with others. Identifying your natural interests and abilities can help you to develop a sense of purpose, and it's this that is most likely to motivate you to work hard and actually have fun while you do it. To have a sense of purpose, you need to know yourself, and what it is you want from your life. Not what others want for you, or what is expected of you, but what actually makes you come alive.

HIDDEN TALENTS

Not all of your attributes will be immediately obvious. Just because you're an Aries, that doesn't mean you always feel brave, for example. You can think about what a typical Aries might be good at, but you are unique, and the stars are only a guide. Think about your strengths – both emotional and physical. The examples on the right might strike a chord with you, or you may want to create your own list.

BECAUSE YOU'RE . . . ADAPTABLE

You are resourceful and like variety. You find it easy to do several tasks at once, and you're a whizz at taking action, even when you don't have a plan.

Maybe you could be a . . .
surgeon, event coordinator, journalist

BECAUSE YOU'RE . . . ENERGETIC

You are a doer more than a thinker and take action to make things happen. Getting things done quickly and efficiently is more important to you than doing something perfectly. You love to achieve things, have bundles of energy and work very hard.

Maybe you could be a . . .
lawyer, soldier, mechanic, driver, estate agent, manager

BECAUSE YOU'RE . . . CREATIVE

You're full of ideas. You love to work imaginatively with ideas or designs and are good at coming up with new ways to do things.

Maybe you could be a . . .
designer, performer, hairdresser, business developer

BECAUSE YOU'RE . . . CARING

You like to work with other people, especially when their wellbeing and development is the focus of your work.

Maybe you could be a . . .
teacher, firefighter, therapist, nurse, charity worker

BECAUSE YOU'RE . . . A LEADER

You love to spend your time persuading other people to do something, buy something or believe in your cause. You're great at influencing and motivating others.

Maybe you could be a . . .
fundraiser, explorer, engineer, entrepreneur

FAMOUS ARIES PEOPLE

Maya Angelou – *poet and civil rights activist*

Lady Gaga – *singer and songwriter*

Leonardo da Vinci – *painter, sculptor, inventor*

Emma Watson – *actor and activist*

Victoria Beckham – *singer and fashion designer*

Vincent van Gogh – *painter*

Harry Houdini – *magician*

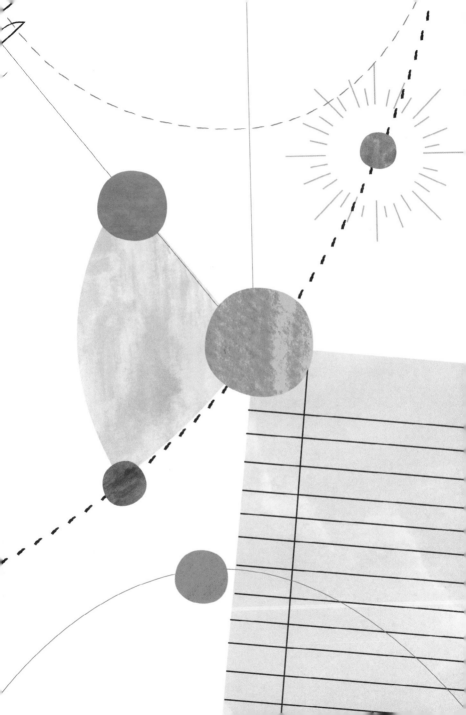

TEAM WORK

Working together with others is essential for almost any career path you choose to follow in later life. School can be competitive, yet working in collaboration with your peers rather than against them builds skills that today's employers are looking for.

Here's how well you work together with ...

ARIES

As you're probably aware by now, Aries can be pretty independent, with some definite ideas about how they want to do things. This means you'll need to take turns doing things your way. The good news is you both like to work at top speed, so your teacher's going to be amazed by how quickly (and well) you complete any set tasks.

TAURUS

Get Taurus on your side and you're on to a winner. Their reliability and patience will be a great balance to your steely determination and enthusiasm. They won't be a pushover – you might need to tread carefully at times and use your best persuasive skills – but once you've won them over, you're likely to make the perfect team.

GEMINI

It might take you a while to get into full team mode, but find your common ground and this pairing can work extremely well. It's bound to be lots of fun, too. Geminis are sociable types and, like you, they thrive in a team situation. Use your confidence to boost theirs, and you'll get lots of great ideas in return.

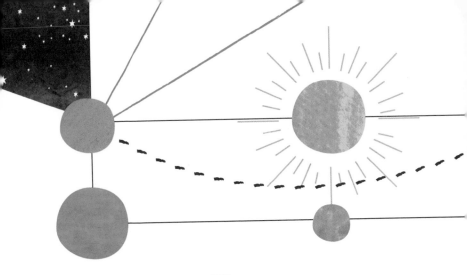

CANCER

You'll probably need to take things at a more gentle pace when working with the crab. You might not immediately see eye to eye, but give them plenty of space to think, respect their emotions and the results could be wonderful. Best of all, once you've earned their loyalty you'll have it for life – or at least until the next argument.

LEO

There won't be any time wasted on getting a task done with you two around. It'll be full throttle all the way, as long as you acknowledge differing opinions and occasionally agree to disagree. Get the balance right and this team will go far, and with plenty of laughter, too.

VIRGO

With their analytical mind, attention to detail, and practical skills, Virgo is a valuable member of any team, and especially for a sometimes impatient Aries. You both have excellent organizational skills, so you will work brilliantly together on big projects and, although not a sucker, Virgo will happily let you take the lead. It's a winning combo.

LIBRA

Diplomatic, level headed and fair-minded, Libra is a great asset to any team. If you're not initially on the same page, take a breath, listen to what they have to say and you should be able to find a compromise. You'll still get the job done – and done well – but it might take a little longer.

SCORPIO

Underneath that cool and calm exterior Scorpios are just as ambitious and determined as you. They're just not as vocal about it. They'll respect your honesty and passion and will watch your back, so it's good to have them on your side, especially if you're working in a competitive environment.

SAGITTARIUS

You both have so much energy and enthusiasm you'll get things done in record time, but try not to rush. It will be easy to get carried away, so make a concerted effort to occasionally stop and make sure you're on the right track, paying closer attention to the detail. Pace yourselves and the results could be wonderful.

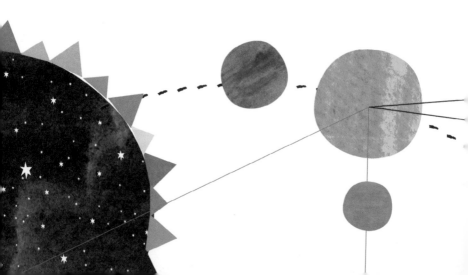

CAPRICORN

While you share an eagerness to succeed, Capricorns tend to take things slow and steady, so your patience might be put to the test at times. However, like you, they love a challenge, especially in the workplace, and will put in 100 per cent effort all the way.

AQUARIUS

Excellent problem solvers and independent thinkers, Aquarians might be just what you need on your team. While you take the lead, they'll be happy to focus on the finer details and might well come up with original ideas that will make all the difference. Give them some freedom and let them surprise you.

PISCES

Creative and imaginative, Pisces are good at thinking outside the box and will bring an extra dimension to any project. They can sometimes be sensitive, so be careful what you say, but they're quick to forgive and are super helpful, and you can rely on them to be just as committed to the task as you are.

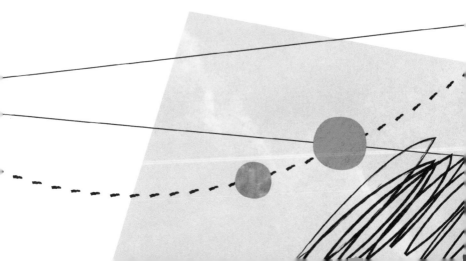

First published 2019
by Ammonite Press
an imprint of Guild of Master Craftsman Publications Ltd
Castle Place, 166 High Street, Lewes, East Sussex, BN7 1XU
United Kingdom

www.ammonitepress.com

Editorial: Susie Duff, Jane Roe, Rachel Roberts, Paul Wade
Designer: Jo Chapman
Illustrations: Sara Thielker
Cover illustration: Sara Thielker

ISBN 978-1-78145-394-0

A catalogue record for this book is available from the British Library

Colour reproduction by GMC Reprographics
Printed and bound in China

AMMONITE
PRESS